PRESENTED TO:

FROM:

THE CISE GUIDE FOR LEADERS

JON WILCOX

Internet addresses given in this book were accurate at the time it went to press.

Printed in the United States of America

Published in Hellertown, PA

Illustrations under license from iStock

ISBN 978-1-952-481-67-3

2 4 6 8 10 9 7 5 3 1 paperback

For more information or to place bulk orders, contact the publisher at Jennifer@BrightCommunications.net.

TO THE
TOP DOG
LEADERSHIP
GROUP

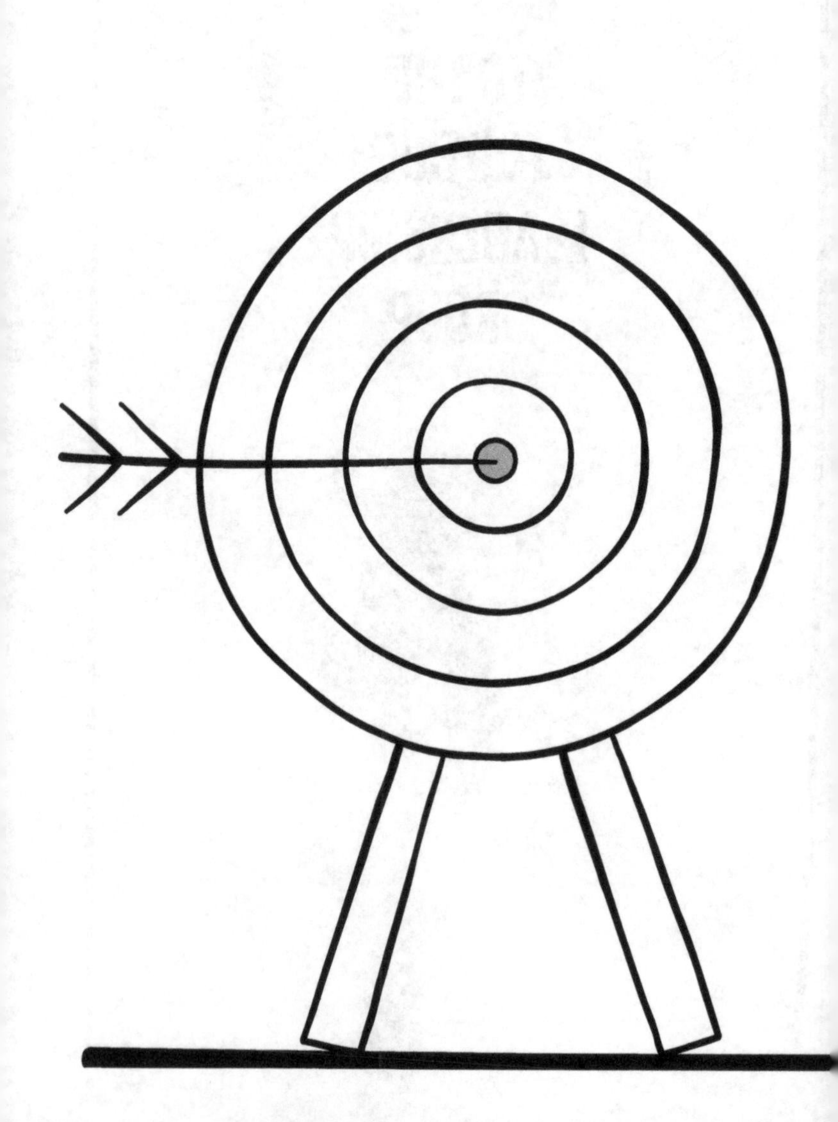

INTRODUCTION

In the old days, you weren't bombarded with text messages and emails. You had time to read letters, and lengthy prose might have been considered smart.

Now, it's best to write with brevity and accuracy. If you don't, your message will likely be deleted.

This book is intended to be like a poster, but in book format. Display it proudly as a conversation piece and a constant reminder to be concise and precise.

Once upon a time,
there was an

INFORMATION OVERLOADED

society.

INFORMATION
INFORMATION
INFORMATION
INFORMATION
INFORMATION
INFORMATION
INFORMATIO
INFORMATION
INFORMATION
INFORMATION
RMATION
MATION
ATION
MATION
ORMATION

That time is

NOW.

The Cise Brothers

OVERPOWERED THE PROBLEM

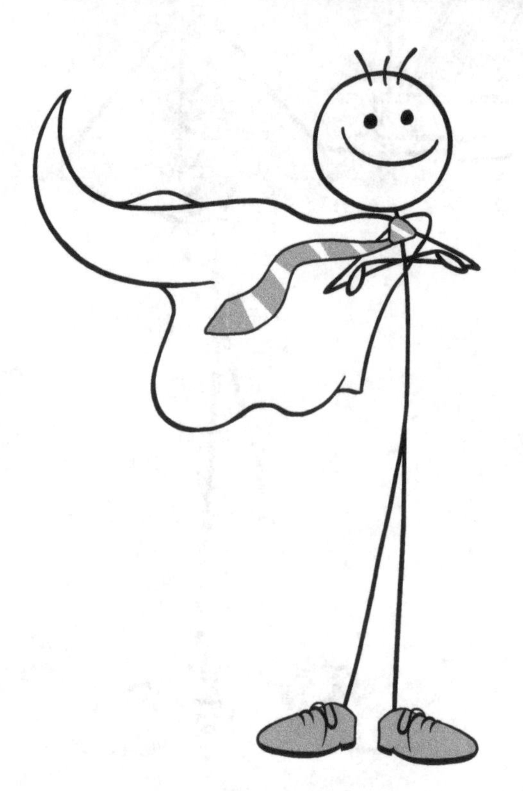

and became

HEROES TO SOCIETY.

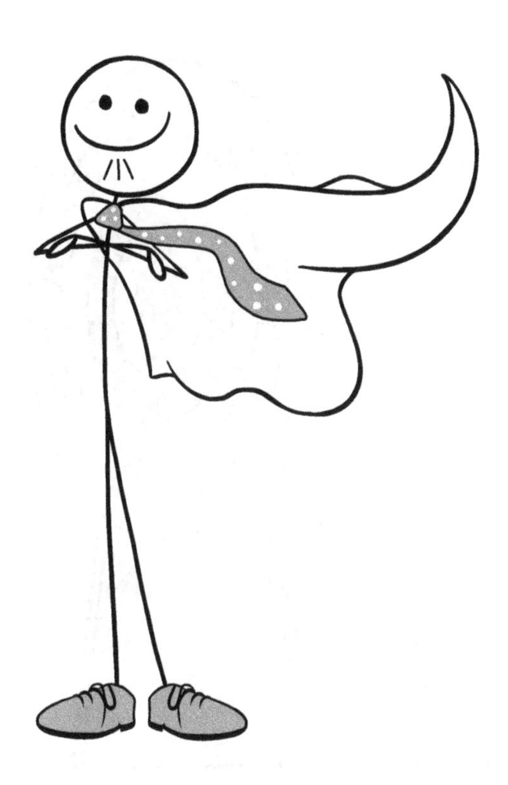

Pre told everyone to be

PRECISE.

Con told
everyone
to be
CONCISE.

TOGETHER,
they are making
the world a
BETTER PLACE.

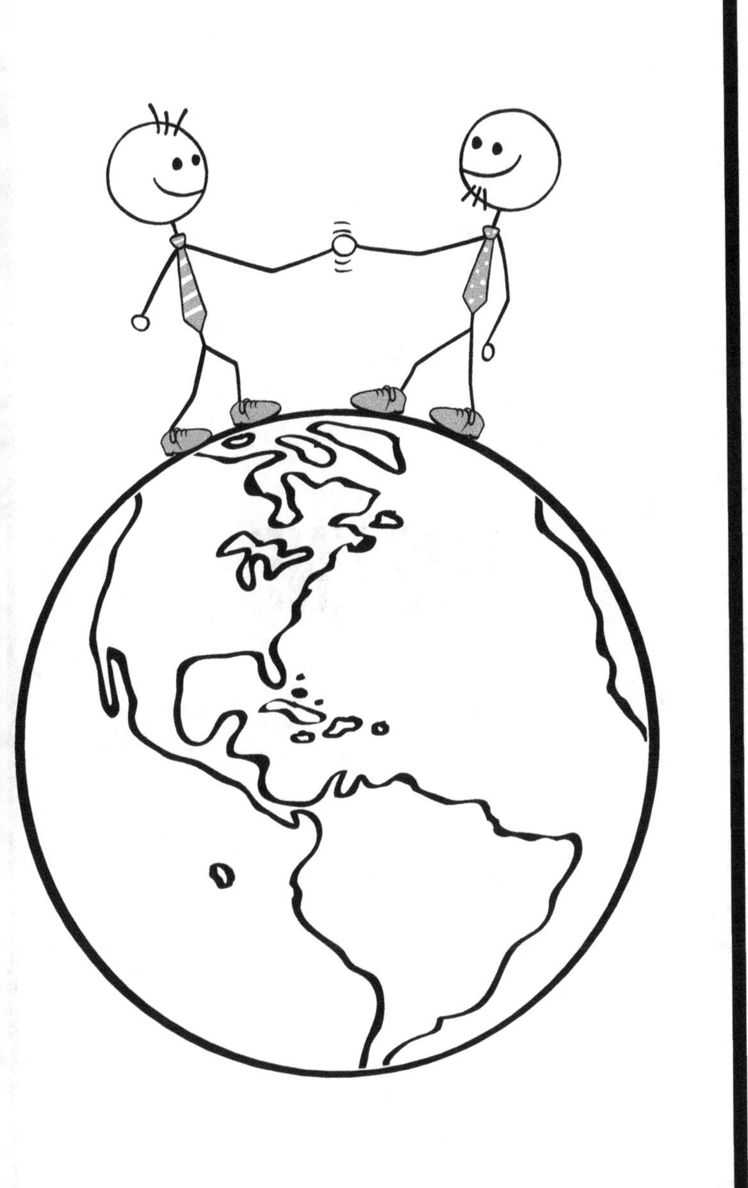

THE END

Start the Conversation

PROUDLY DISPLAY YOUR BOOK

Display on a stand

Or simply stand upright on a desk

Or hang on a wall

NOTES

ABOUT THE AUTHOR

Jon Wilcox has enjoyed a diversified engineering career, including working on industrial air pollution controls, robotics, fighter aircraft fuel controls, and hydraulic systems that lifted rockets up to the launch pad.

After 25 years in industry, Jon changed his career to help people buy and sell their most valuable assets, real estate, currently in Pennsylvania and Florida.

One of Jon's passions is leadership, and he wants to help people learn valuable lessons so that they can enjoy better careers.

Jon earned a bachelor's degree in mechanical engineering from Lehigh University and a master's degree in business from Rensselaer Polytechnic University (RPI).

For more information: visit
www.TopDogLeadership.Life

CPSIA information can be obtained
at www.ICGtesting.com
Printed in the USA
BVHW061114021221
623077BV00002B/201